The Power Of Love
My Personal Notes

Written By Jaja Soze

Copyright 2020 Jaja Soze

The author asserts the moral right under the Copyright, Design and Patents Act 1988 to be identified as the author of this work.

All rights reserved. No part of this publication may be reproduced, stored in a retrieval system or transmitted, in any form or by any means without the prior written consent of the author, nor be otherwise circulated in any form of binding or cover other than that in which it is published and without a similar condition being imposed on the subsequent purchaser.

www.jajasoze.com

Photography by: Karina Lidia

Cover design and art work by: Kavi Shah

Edited by: Jane Oriel

Contents

10 **Baby in the Jungle**

18 Hugs and Kisses

24 Me And Her

32 **A Battle in the Mind**

35 Koba and Ceaser Love

38 Just Random

42 **What a year its been**

52 How do you find yourself

56 The Balance/God and the Devil

61 **Dysfunction Part 1**

62 The Magic of Music

64 Her

70 **My Brother the street**

75 The Interview

82 Dysfunction part 2

88 **Think Great**

94 Random head moment

96 insecurities

96 **The inner voice or intuition**

98 Forgiveness

104 Be Great Be the F* Greatest

Acknowledgements

I Express special thanks and Love:
To My family and friends

The Power of Love

Forward

A body and mind without love is an empty body and mind: My journey so far in life has been a difficult one, and I have come to understand that my difficulty was mostly to do with the fact that I was growing up and moving forward without love.

Many people from the streets and inner-city culture have grown up with this same burden and a belief that love is soft and non-progressive, not realising this same mentality is what holds us back in life in the first place.

One of the most powerful gifts we have been given as human beings is the gift of love. I don't mean your average soppy kiss in the movies type of love, or the random, *I love you* kind of love. The love I'm talking about is a deep inner-soul love, the love that connects all your inner chakras together, then spreads an energy outside of you that is beautiful and peaceful.

Love connects people, love inspires and motivates, love makes things happen. I used to think love was like when a lost young boy on the streets feels left out and lonely and he picks up his first gun and suddenly feels like he has a friend, someone who will understand him help and guide him, cleaning the gun every day and smiling at the gun feeling loved and protected. That used to be my love.

I want to bring you on a journey of how that same little boy found a new love.

Be Great, Be The F**cking Greatest.

Introduction

The purpose of this book is to bring you into my world and mindset, to give you a better understanding of your local thug, your community leader, your estate don, the guy you always see getting stopped and searched by the police, the guy you always see on the news for murdering another guy that was just like him, and the people who are trying to build something great from absolutely nothing at all.

This will help you have a better understanding of the young girl who had no father in her life to guide her, and tell her how beautiful she is and how amazing her hair is, and that one day but not now, she will be a mother and inspiration to some of her own beautiful and amazing children.
Why are these people so angry? Why are they so self-destructive?

It's because the world has displaced, misdirected, and miseducated them. They have grown up in a world of no love, no self-worth and no identity. But I believe, if we connect with love our powers as human beings will be reignited and we will be able to access our highest potentials.

When you can differentiate between ego and your true self then you will be able to access love more easily.
Whether you are a local estate goon, a single mother or a college professor, I want you to follow my journey and ideas and experiences of how I see and feel the power of love.

Chapter 1

A baby in the jungle: If you put a baby in an empty room with biscuits and a pile of shit (yeah, real shit manure), after the baby eats all the biscuits and cries, the baby will put his hand in the shit and lick it off because the baby has not been told that shit is horrible and not for consumption. The baby has not been programmed or controlled yet, so the baby will make up its own mind. If the baby thinks the shit tastes okay, the baby will continue to lick the shit. If the baby hates the taste, it will most probably cry, crawl away and eventually fall asleep. But when the baby wakes up and cries again and is really hungry the baby is more than likely going to return to the shit and put it in its mouth.

Again, if a newborn baby is put into a jungle, it will eventually learn to live like the animals in the jungle. It will learn from the animals and copy their patterns and habits. The baby will grow to adore the jungle and love the jungle, the baby will become desensitised to the dangers of the jungle, and in return will grow up just as dangerous as its wild surroundings.
At the same time, the baby will learn how to adapt to the loyalty and rules of the wild animals and learn their codes of conduct.
Now, if you take that baby who is now a young adult (let's say, 21 years old), and you bring him to a new human city just like a Jungle Book, or Tarzan, or another "jungle dude goes to the city" type corny movie, you will see that this will take a lot of retraining, education, emotional and language barrier rehabilitation, to bring his character and mindset to that of a normal human being (whatever that means), but you get what I mean, hopefully.

I gave you this concept because this is what happens to a lot the young people on the streets, including myself. We have been brought up in a dysfunctional jungle, we start off as being part of a lion and lioness family set up, but Dad ends up leaving to date a gorilla, and Mum is left raising the babies by herself. And therefore, we are unbalanced, in unhappy and, if not poor, struggling households.

Seeing this daily makes a young person bitter, revenge-driven, motivated by anger and with a lust for material possessions and an attitude of, *I'm going to show the world who I am!*

I remember growing up on the streets of Handsworth in Birmingham UK, and running around as a young Rastafarian with a love in me that was so big it made me shine. It made me popular amongst my peers, I made lots of friends, and I was rarely in any stress.

I must have been about six or seven years old and I was mischievous and adventurous and got into trouble a few times but I was happy and I had a sense of love in my energy. I look back at this time in my life and wonder to myself why was I so happy and filled with love, what was so special about this time in my life? For years I couldn't figure it out, then it came to me one day. The reason I felt happy and a sense of love was because I didn't have any negative attachments, I didn't have any negative worries, I was just living, learning and growing. I was free to roam, free to discover, free to ask, free to have any type of friends; black, white, Asian and so on.

Because of this free spirit vibe, I had been able to tap into love and happiness without realising I was doing it. I was like that baby in a jungle, but I was not scared to adapt and grow.

So, if we start out as young babies and children with a natural energy of love for people and the world around us, why do we later in life abandon this energy and replace it with fear and ignorance? What influences our energy to forget about love?

The baby in the jungle is willing to love and grow and make friends, but on the journey, the baby shows love and affection to a tiger because he believes everyone is a friend and the jungle is a warm, friendly place. When he goes to hug and greet the tiger, the tiger bites him hard, the baby screams in agony and tries to run away.

The tiger, looking menacing and evil, chases the baby and pounces forward. The baby is just about to get savaged when a large snake lands in front of the tiger and pierces him in the neck with its poisonous venom. The tiger growls and runs off into the jungle, leaving behind a scared and crying baby.

The snake is a cunning and deceptive creature and wants to eat the baby just as much as the tiger, but not right away, so instead the snake pretends to protect the baby, to give the baby a false sense of love. The baby is now grateful for the snake being so brave and saving his life. The young child is now starting to experience that not all the animals in the jungle are nice. He now thinks all tigers are horrible and mean, and that all snakes are amazing protectors of the jungle and are his friend.

As time passes, the baby and the snake move across the jungle. The snake teaches the baby cunning and deceptive behaviours and techniques so the baby can survive. The snake tells the baby that all the animals in the jungle are dangerous and will want to eat him.

The snake says the jungle hates babies, which makes the baby upset and wonder why the animals hate him when he hasn't done any harm. The young human cries until the pain turns to anger, then to hate, then finally he is filled with a new energy of rage.

The snake sees this rage and realises it will be more beneficial to keep the baby alive now, because the baby's rage can help to feed and finance the snake's greedy needs. So the snake, wanting to rule the monkey's turf and tree area of the jungle, tells the baby that the monkeys are planning to kill the baby, so together the snake and the baby create an amazing plan to hijack, and kill the monkeys.

All this time the baby thinks he is doing something good, but he has no more love energy, so is thinking and acting purely out of rage and anger, not realising he is only being used by the snake, and that in fact the monkeys are harmless and have no intention of killing the baby.

So, bring this back into reality, the jungle would be society, the baby would be you and me, the tiger would be other lost people, the snake would be the system, and the monkeys would be your real friends, partners and family who love you, but who you hurt the most.

This is how we are misguided and misdirected through the jungle as babies. We learn and are taught that love is an enemy, the snake is constantly telling us to create egos, fear and to hurt others, show no love and trust no one.

These concepts are the tools we go on to carry throughout our lives. Tragically, we then pass these same habits and lessons on to our children, which continues to create the cycle of a baby in a jungle.

Believe in yourself

Chapter 2

Hugs and kisses:
As a young child I never received loads of hugs and kisses from my parents. I grew up in a revolutionary household, very strong and cultured, where I was taught to be strong amongst a world of racism and no equal rights. It started with 4 or 5 hugs as a baby, 4 or 3 hugs as a child, 2 or 1 hug as an 11 year old and after that it was non-existent. That lack of love and affection from my family affected my whole life, and relationships especially. Up to this day I find it awkward when someone tries to hug me.

On the streets, many of us grew up in similar households with a lack of love expressed or shown in our families. To compensate, we brought that same energy out and into our environment, causing many of us internal and external emotional problems.

I remember when I was about 12 years old and I was going through some regular street stress, and I just wanted someone to hold me, hug me and say, *Elijah, I love you, everything will be OK*, but damn, that never happened. So I just said fuck love, fuck being emotional, I've got to have my own back. Feeling like this made me create within myself an ego character who many know today as Jaja Soze.

It's like I yearned for love so much and yet I didn't receive none, so I became desensitised to love. Most of my friends were experiencing the same thing so we instantly had something in common, and in that similarity we then created our own warped version of love, like a street type of love, like a group of orphans who watched out for each other.

11

Why was it so hard for me and other young people on the streets to receive hugs and love from our family and peers? Why did the streets want us to be so hard and unloved? It was like the streets raised soldiers to fight a war, but what war? The war was mainly within us, we were fighting against each other, we were killing ourselves.

I asked my Mum about this one day, and she was a bit dismissive about the whole subject, but she also told me, that she too didn't receive many hugs or love from her Mum and Dad. So, I guess she passed on the baton of no hugs and love to me.

Me and my Mum's bond was more like big sister and little brother, a very cool big sister who had permission to act the Mum role, lol. This was probably due to the fact my Mum gave birth to me when she was very young, so I also watched her grow at the same time.

My Mum was my hero, she was super cool and she understood my hunger to explore and grow and let me do my thing, but with a couple broomstick beatings here and there, and also when I got out of order or got brought home by the police, which was very regular.

Anyway, so back to the whole hug thing. The other day my oldest daughter Kenya, who is now 9 years old, said to me, *Dad you don't really hug me anymore, do you still love me?*

Wow, I could have cried a million times, fainted and cried some more. That's how hard her words hit me. Was I about to continue and pass the baton of no hugs and love on to my children?

I told her that I really loved her and that she, along with her brothers and sisters, are the joys of my life – well, most of the time anyway.

And I explained to her that my life has been very difficult and I've been through some tough times, so sometimes I don't express the love to her as I probably should, but I made sure I reassured her by saying that I loved her unconditionally, and I hope and pray she believed me.

I can now see how badly I have been affected by the attitude and principles of the streets, by dismissing the power of love.

I remember thinking that the streets loved me, and the people on the streets had genuine love and respect for me.

I thought I could count on them all the time, and this is why I was so loyal to the streets, the blocks, the pavements. This was my love.

It would take some serious mistakes and experiences to happen in my life, for me to later realise that it was all an illusion, it was all a lie.

I mean, how can anyone love you if they don't even know what the energy of love is? We are just like hamsters, all in one box running on a big wheel, going around in circles in a continuous negative cycle.
And because we are all in the box together, we create this illusion of a loving family, when really and truly, everyone just wants to get out the box and live their own lives.
Because if it was really love, we would see the hurt and pain in what we are doing, and we would work together to try and break us all out the box and make sure our children never have to enter the restraints of that same box.
Instead, we re-create the negative big wheel for our children to run around in the same continuous circle. This is because we are not thinking or building with love, we are thinking and building with anger, greed and hostility towards a system that was created for us to fail.

We are focusing our energy in the wrong directions.
For this cycle to change in our communities, we must first understand that love is the foundation we need to start from, self-love, love of self, love of family, love for your community, love for life, love of the world.

You can start today by giving your children, partner, family a big random hug, regardless of any issues. Start a new vibe with them, create a new energy and frequency with them. That simple hug could change the foundations of how they think and feel.

Chapter 3

Me And Her: One day when I was younger, my girlfriend came to hug me and while she gave me a hug she whispered, *I love you*. I didn't know how to act, and I felt awkward, how do I respond to that?

If I'd said I love you back, I'd be lying coz I didn't know what love was, haven't felt love or been given any love for a long time, I was lost. And if I'd say I don't love you, she would be upset. But it was the truth, I was cold, I had abandoned love years ago. I grew up close to anger and stubbornness and aggression. I was hard, tough, I had street credibility, I was from the hood, the block, and I don't do love.

I bought her flowers a couple of times, but that wasn't because I loved her; that was just because I had seen people give their girlfriends flowers on TV, movies, adverts etc., so I knew that's what I was supposed to do.

I was basically being a sheep. I didn't follow my heart because hearts 'n' stuff was associated with girls, and I was busy being ruthless.

I'd been affected by the lack of love I had received growing up, and in turn it made me disassociate from love in my relationships.

My partner one day asked if I would ever get married, and in my head I was like, *Is she mad? What, and only have one woman? No way! And be sitting watching TV with her for the rest of my life?* That was like an ultimate nightmare. I associated that with going to prison.

But all I said to her was, *Well, maybe one day*, without hurting her feelings.

I didn't tell her that I wanted loads of women, cars, money and houses. I associated love with having one woman, kids, getting a job and living a boring life watching EastEnders and Coronation Street. Damn! That was a scary thought and I wanted no part in that scenario.

Meanwhile for her, it was not that she was more emotionally mature than me. She had her own demons, and she had also grown up in a dysfunctional family. Her father was in her life but in the background (and when I say background, I mean like the black guy in the pub in EastEnders, who just speaks now again).

So, for her, I believe she saw love as the father figure she didn't have in her life. She subconsciously saw me as the father figure she didn't have, but always wanted, and she believed and associated that vibe with love.

But how can you search for a father figure in a lost boyfriend who is the male version of herself? We were both lost souls searching for things neither of us understood.

And imagine, In that process of chaos children can be created; not out of love but out of horny sex, and because of this, the cycle of confusion continues.

I was chilling one day with one of my "old skool" girlfriends and I asked her, *Do you love yourself?* She looked at me baffled, and she said, *Yeah, of course I do.*

So I said, *When you wake up in the morning with no makeup, no eyebrows done, do you love that person?* She still wasn't getting it and said defiantly, *Yeah!*
So I said, *Well why don't you show that person that you love to the world?*, and she quickly replied, *I do!*

I quickly returned with, *No you don't! You never leave your house without a wig; do you not like your hair? You never leave your house without makeup, do you not like your face?* She looked a bit upset and said, *It's because I look better with these things but I'm still beautiful without them.*

Then I said, *Why not show the world the beauty you wake up with, why not balance it out?*

P.s (i am not saying make up is a bad thing by the way).

Anyway, She thought about it for a while and said, *You know what, I don't like what I see when I wake up, I think I look horrible.*

*So now you see, you do **not** love yourself, you are just like me.* I used to wake up, and instead of learning to love who I am, I focused straight on the negatives.

This is why we are creating problems in our day to day life, because we start our days with a negative energy. We wake up every day hating who we are, and go through life trying to be like what society tells us is nice or successful.

This is not love, this is us feeding into our ego energy, and is why we are so angry most of the time because we are walking alongside energies such as lust, envy, hate, greed, or jealousy. Imagine how destructive it can be when a male and female, both from the streets who have come from dysfunctional backgrounds, start to have a relationship and they are both working off negative energies.

It's chaos, and creates no space for growth, and most of these types of relationships consist of daily arguments, cheating, smoking weed, more arguing, pregnancies, more weed, prison, cheating and it goes on and on in a cycle of non-progression, until their child grows up to be a rapper, pissed off, and makes songs explaining all the above in detail. Damn what a life!

It's deep. I mean how can you love someone else, if you don't already love yourself? You need to love yourself, feel it, understand it, nurture love, care for it, and build on it. Once you can feel the growth of love inside yourself, you can then share the love with others. But if you do not have love, then how can you share it? You cannot share or give something that you do not have, or intend to get. It just doesn't make sense.

I look at my woman and I think, *Damn she's sexy! Look at the arse, cor blimey, that is wonderful, oh shit, and the breasts are amazing, and I can't wait to have sex with her later!* I looked at her from a low-frequency angle, because I myself at the time, was thinking like that, also on a low-frequency level.

For me to value my woman I must first value myself, my mum, my sister etc.., then I'll be able to show that same value and respect to my woman.

See, if I look at my woman from a love angle, I start thinking really different. Instead, my focus goes onto her personality, her traits, her amazing and beautiful aura, the way she touches things and smiles, the way her eyes light up when she sees me. Everything changes now! Your woman, your queen becomes almost magical, extraordinary. That's how powerful love is when you implement it into how you think about her.

Sometimes your two eyes can deceive you, maybe its time to use your hidden one.

Chapter 4

A Battle In The Mind:
From a young age, I was a deep thinker; sometimes perhaps a bit too deep when I would scare myself. I'd have dreams every night without fail, vivid, in-depth dreams when I slept, then throughout the day I would think deep. It's completely exhausting and I'm often very tired, not including all the dramas of my life that come once I wake up, it's like a constant battle.

When you have delved deep into the street culture, it affects your mind-state. The experience of constant crime, disorder, guns and drugs, shoot outs, friends dying, prison and family dysfunction, is enough to send anyone to a mental institution. Furthermore some of my closest friends and family are sitting in mental institutions as I write this.

Sometimes I think to myself, am I one thought away from going mental? Sometimes I get flashbacks of robberies I've done, and the scared look on the people's faces haunts me. It's like a part of me, the dark ego, wants to be famous, and rich, and popular and fuck lots of women, and buy guns, and do crazy shit every day. Then there's the light, meditative part of me, that wants to help and heal people, build communities, start a revolution, find and spread the message of love.

And every day these two argue a constant battle. The ego is like, *Why are you being nice? Nice people do not make money or get successful. Fuck all that nice shit, let's grab the guns go outside and make some money. Once you make money, you can fuck all the nice bitches easily, truss me we need power.*

And my light side is like, *Nah come, let's meditate and get rid of the ego, let's build in peace, write poetry and make love to one beautiful woman and give guidance to your children, and money will follow automatically.*

One thing that I had to learn over the years, was that a person must find balance because you need both light and dark energies; one cannot work without the other, you need total balance. Ignoring one energy and living only in the other is unrealistic and unbalanced.

There was a time in my life when I was only in touch with my dark side. I had money, cars, and popularity but I wasn't happy. And there was also a time when I was in touch with my light side. I had religion, prayer, meditation, and met a whole load of people who had the gift of the gab with knowledge but no willingness to physically put it into action. It was basically all talk and no action and I was definitely unhappy, because I'm an activist, meaning I need to be involved in real active work.

So, over the years I started mixing the two to create balance while utilising both options and energies to form one unique vibe and personality. But I realised that to make this work I would need to harness one important element for me to fully become one with myself, and that my people, was Love.

The mind is amazing, but is also a slave to whatever you feed it.
Give the mind negativity and it adapts to help you bring in more negativity. So feed your mind greatness, positivity and countless love, and by default it will return the same energy back into your life.

Chapter 5

Koba and Caesar Love

Growing up, I had some very close friends that I thought would be with me until the end of days, but how wrong was that theory!

One friend (I won't mention his name just in case he's broke and tries to sue me. I ain't got time for all that). Anyway, he was a normal, cool guy, so I brought him around me, and he became extra cool and popular. I thought he was a good-hearted guy. How wrong was I, once again.

All the time I was making money and just being me, he was secretly hating on me and plotting on my downfall. He wanted to be like me so badly that he started to hate my guts. Instead of working on himself and concentrating on his own individual growth and progress, he was too busy focusing on my life; how sad is that!

I call this Koba and Caesar love, like in the film *The Planet of the Apes*. Koba has been held and terrorised by the humans in a medical facility. Eventually, he is freed by Caesar and his company. He goes to live in the forest with the apes, and Caesar helps them all, guides them, and builds a new home and society for them.

At first Koba is all good and is Caesar's number one right-hand man, but when the humans try to come back around them, Koba gets upset. Caesar tells him to just cool, he's got this, and him being the leader, he will sort it out. To cut a long story short, Koba betrays and tries to kill Caesar so he can be the new leader and run the pack. Basically, Koba was secretly plotting to take out Caesar the whole time.

He was pretending to be loyal, with plans to take Caesar's position. This same thing happens on the streets every day, and many so-called friendships are based around this same concept of disloyalty.

I used to always be baffled at why these people are like this? Why are they such cowards, and where does all the deception come from?

It comes down to love. You're thinking how can love be involved in this type of disloyalty?

OK, well the Kobas of the world have a big urge for love and attention like the rest of us, and they see how much people love and respect the Caesars of the world, and they want the same. But instead of learning, gaining knowledge, good respect, manners and growing to gain real love, the Kobas want to skip all of that and just take all the love the Caesars of the world have and take it for themselves.

And the Kobas of the world will do anything to be loved including killing their friends and family.
To them, *they* are doing no wrong and think everyone else is weak.

This is the typical mindset of a coward.

I call this the **Koba and Caesar love.**

Just Random: One day I woke up from a good night's sleep, and felt rejuvenated, motivated and inspired.
I said *Today, I'm going to do something different, I'm going to do something out of the ordinary.*

So, I showered, put on some clothes and walked towards my car. Usually, I would have just jumped in the car and drove off (that's what I always do) but today I'm being different, so I smiled, put my keys back in my pocket and walked to the Train station.

I walked slowly on my way there, and watched everything, and everyone in detail, and thought to myself,

I wonder if these people feel loved?

I got to the train station, bought a ticket, went down the escalator and waited on the platform for the train that was due to arrive in four minutes.

While waiting, I just stared at everyone. No one on the platform looked happy, everyone looked pissed off, with the I've-been-forced-out-of-my-bed type of face.
I wanted to go over to a lady standing a few feet from me and say, *Hey what's up, how you doing, do you feel loved today?*

But then I thought I better not just in case she thinks I'm a perv and tries to punch me in the face.
Anyway, the train arrives, and I wait for all the people to rush off, and I walk on board and take a seat, and other people start sitting and standing.

I just look around and think *Damn, not one person is smiling, how cannot one person be smiling? Where is the love?*

I stand up and move to the side, find a safe spot and just observe the whole place. Everyone looks angry, (well maybe that's a bit of an exaggeration, but it was the majority).
I stood there observing different people, thinking to myself, wondering what that person is thinking, or I wonder what kinda life that guy has, etc.

Well eventually, I plucked up the courage - not that I lack courage, but me being an alpha male of African heritage in central London, trying to approach random people can easily go wrong.

So anyway, I saw this old-ish kinda guy and said *Excuse me can I have a word?* He looked at me puzzled, and said, *Sure, how can I help?*

I replied, *When's the last time you said, "I love you" to someone?*

He said, *This morning. I said "I love you" to my wife before leaving.*

I said *OK, that's nice but did you mean it when you said it?*

He looked puzzled, then said, *Yeah, well kind of, as it's in my usual morning routine.*

He paused for a second looking at me, then thinking, he said, *You know what, I'm going to call my wife right now, and tell her that I really love her, and appreciate her!* He took out his phone and called her, and as she answered, he shook my hand, smiled and walked away.

What he had just realised was, he was saying, I love you to his wife out of convenience and routine, but there was no real meaning behind it.

Many of us do this daily. We say I love you without meaning it, with no strength behind it, no vibration or frequency. We say it because it sounds good and is often expected of us.

Chapter 6

What a year it's been

For me, 2017 was one of the hardest years of my life, to date. It was my transformation year from boy to a man and damn, was it a hard one!

I had put myself into debt, I had to sell my car, my motorbike and a few other bits just so I could maintain myself throughout the year. My bank balance went to zero, I nearly lost my flat, my music studio, and my sanity.

All my close friends had vanished over the years, so I didn't expect help or support from any of them because most of them were just sheep, anyway. Over the years, experiences like this have made me grow, expand and realise my true potential, and I have been able to learn from the struggles life has thrown at me. Most of the struggles I faced were because I made some bad choices in my business and personal life, but I never gave up. Each time, I just started again and learned from my mistakes.

There were times when I wanted to go and rob a bank but I thought against it as that was me going back in time, and that's not a progressive move. Plus, I don't think I've got any more energy to sit in a cell for 23 hours a day, eating potato and wet steamed chicken. I would also miss my children way too much. And no sex - that's a defo no to prison life!

This past year has made me look into myself and my personality, my past life and my future. 2017 made me ask myself important questions like, who are you? Where are you going? What do you value? Do you love yourself? Do you understand love? Why are these people around you? Sometimes we forget to sit back and have a reality check and look deeper into our lives, and 2017 made me look into myself like never before.

You see, things don't always go as planned. The Universe, God, Allah, the Source, or whatever fancy name you prefer, wants you to grow and learn in the process, because how can you get up and become a better person if you are not falling down and making mistakes?
Sometimes we humans make choices and go in directions based on our dysfunctional and social media, TV-type mindsets. For example, a man will look at a woman and think, *Yes, she is beautiful. I love her and I'm going to marry her.*

He doesn't realise it at the time but he has based his assumption on looking at her breasts, her bum, and her face full of make-up (I'm assuming she has make-up on. If she hasn't, then all feminists, before you punch me in the face, please except my sincere apologies). Anyway, he is basing his love on the woman's outside appearance, but later down he will go to the woman's house and find the house is a tip, she talks behind all her friends' backs, and her personality sucks.

So now, he is in a relationship with this woman and he's unhappy, in that moment the universe will send another woman into his life who is the opposite of what he thought was beautiful, and this new woman will not be fancy dressed.

She will have a nice shaped body but not like the Instagram body he lusts over, and he will notice the new woman's personality is amazing and she makes him realise that he needs to change his mindset and choices. But this new woman with the amazing personality will already be in a relationship and not interested in him. The universe does shit like that to teach us a lesson.

Right, now I'm in Morocco sitting on a sofa with big cushions, looking at the beautiful trees and listening to the birds speaking to each other, and I'm wondering what they are saying. I'm also letting my thoughts drift where they want to.

Random Thought #1
Don't you think it's crazy how the Western World say their way of life is the best, yet they have the unhappiest people living there?

Random Thought #2
Anyway, I was thinking, (I think quite a lot, as you can probably tell), when people say they understand or overstand love, do they really, though?

Why I say this is because if we say we love our girlfriend or boyfriend, do you then also love their mum and Dad, and then do you also love the higher source that created the mum and the Dad? Also, when you take the person you love to an amazing beach and they adore you for it, do you also love nature for its beauty and for allowing you access to explore it and to be adored?

My point is, you can't just take bits of love and leave the rest because it will leave you incomplete. You must take love, and love as a whole.
For example, if you like oranges, you really, really love oranges, but if you love oranges you have to love and respect the tree that grows the oranges. Then, you must love and respect the soil that gives the tree life, and then you have to love and respect the sun and water that help the soil to flourish and give life, so you have to love the whole process in order to fully, really love and respect the orange.
For a man to love a woman, he must also love her faults, her failures, her inner darkness and light, her mum her Dad, her story, her cycle, and her direct connection with nature and the universe. He must love her as a whole, and in return the woman must also love the man as a whole.

Many people come into our lives, and I don't believe any come as being simply good or bad. I believe people come into our lives to help us learn, and to help us to look more into ourselves. They also come to help us to improve or to inspire and help others.

When it's time to move on from the people currently around us, the universe will send new people to us depending on the frequency we are sending out to the universe. So, when certain types of people come into our lives, instead of looking at the situation as being either good or bad, look at it this way.

What is the universe trying to tell me? What does it want me to see or learn?

Sometimes, the people who come into your life that you regard as bad, could really be a reflection of yourself, and the universe wants you to experience how you behave through someone else, so you can see yourself more clearly and make changes.

The universe, higher source, God etc. does not speak English or broken Jamaican slash London slang. Instead, the universe will send people, incidents, coincidences, messages in dreams, visions, prayer, repeat numbers etc., to communicate with us and help direct and guide each one of us. The reason why it is so hard for us to read these signs, is because society also throws its fair share at us to help confuse and misdirect us away from this universal language.

For instance, it's going to be hard to read universal messages when you're worrying about your next council tax and business rates bills.
The social constructs we live in have put so much pressure on us that we now live in constant fear and worry. This in return puts each of us on a thinking frequency that is low and negative, which makes it near impossible to free-think or see clearly.

So, I would advise you all to take regular breaks to quiet parks, fields, mountains, hills, beaches which will give you the space to clear the mind and body from the social poison that we must live with daily. Even just an hour or two out of your normal life can make a difference.
#JustSayin'

One day, when everyone you are with is talking, don't join the conversation, just listen carefully and acknowledge what is being said. Pay attention to not only what is being said, but **how** it is being said. Look at the attitudes of the people speaking, look at their body language, you will learn a lot more this way.

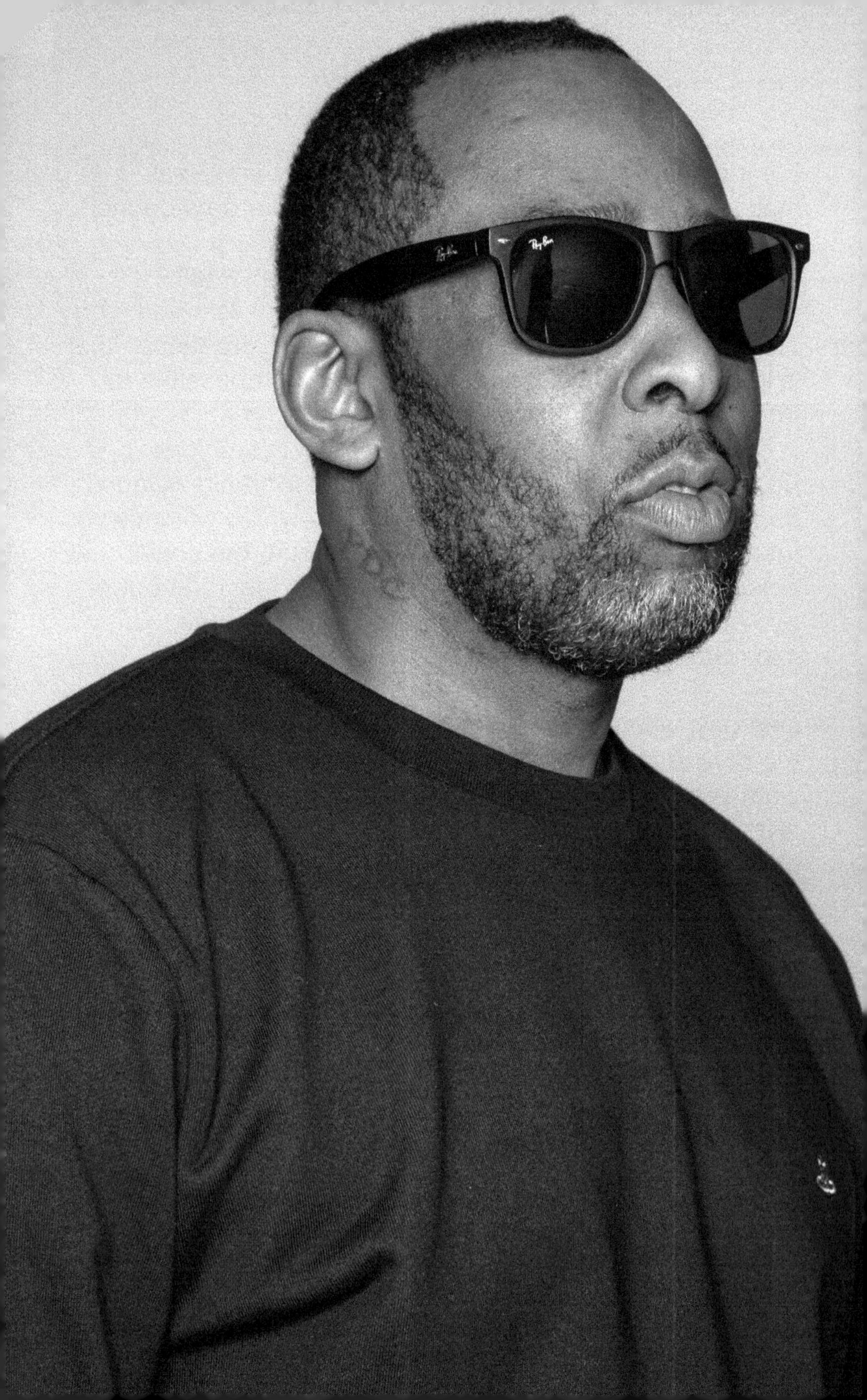

We were confused lonely and fell in love with a firearm.

Street love.

The other day I was with some friends they were all speaking about making money blah blah blah, so this time, I just stayed quiet and listened and watched. The richest person in the room spoke and gave some good advice on making money, his opinion on people who are broke etc., but he was quickly and loudly interrupted by the person with the least money in the room but who looked the richest. This person spoke loudly and made sure everyone heard him and he got his point across, but whenever someone else tried to speak he would interrupt them, and speak over everyone.

Now, as I'm watching him speak, I notice he looks angry, yet the conversation at this point has been about progress and how to inspire. As I'm watching him I can see he feels intimidated and insecure, because deep down he knows he is acting fake, pretending to be someone he is not. I see him growing angry with himself for trying to keep up with his own lie, so soon he changes the conversation to guns and drugs and his past street life because this brings the conversation to a time when he was the man, he had street credibility and lots of money etc.

He feels fulfilled now, talking about the past, but he gets angry when the conversation is about current life or future topics, so is he really being truthful to himself? Instead of living a current lie pretending he's living great, he should be putting focus on the fact that he is not really doing well and how he could change it for the better in order to see new progress.

So, while he's chatting away, I'm just sitting here listening like I'm Kermit the Frog drinking tea.

Chapter 7

How do you find yourself? Yes, I'm random. I
write what I want, when I want and in no particular order. That's what makes being a free thinker so great.

You see, society and the powerful human beings that we see as the ones who run the world really dislike free thinkers. They prefer sheep people because people who follow and don't question, make it easier for them to rule (I don't want my book to get banned, so I'll go easy on them for now). Anyway, to truly be at peace with yourself and to find out who you really are, you have to strip yourself bare, right back to basics (I don't mean strip your clothes off and go walking down the street - even though you could do that if you wanted to). I mean letting go of all material things, all bondages, fake friends and family, damaging relationships, religion, media influence, TV; basically, all the shit society throws at us, you need to cut it all out.

I'm not saying you can't go back to some of these things, because balance is always needed, but to begin your journey of finding yourself, you must start from the basic form of yourself, stripped bare.

Go someplace where you will not be distracted, turn your phone off or leave it at home. I would say go away by yourself for a month, minimum. During the first week, just chill out and do absolutely nothing, just relax your mind, sleep, eat and drink lots of fresh water. For the second week stay relaxed but now start to look at your life, past and current. Take a look at who have you become, are you happy, are you in a good place in life, do you have good friends and family, do they motivate you, who are you? Ask yourself many questions, truthful questions, and be honest with yourself.

On week three, meditate, pray. Don't ask for anything; instead just meditate in silence, listen and watch the chaos in your mind. Keep on doing this throughout the week until you escape and settle the chaotic mind, now you will have access to speak to yourself and have a conversation with your inner child, your soul, your source.

What happens during or after this point is totally up to you. Everyone's journey will be different. When week four comes, relax, enjoy being the new you, but make sure you do monthly getaways on a regular basis as the chaos can come right back to haunt you if you're not on point.

We are taught from a very young age to conform. They give us a list say pick an occupation. We pick one, then they say OK now work hard at it, and we do, then get stressed, marry people we don't love, have kids we don't always want (but end up appreciating them regardless), and then we die (flipping heck that sounded depressing just thinking about it).

So really, we don't have a free will choice, but we are given systematically built options. It's like we're given a limited choice of pre-made ready meals.

But what if I don't want your horrible half-cooked ready meal, what if I want to cook my own meal, with my own ingredients and my own outcome, what then?
Why didn't school teach me how to survive without no money, and also how to travel the world with hardly any money? These choices and practices would have put many of us on a much better journey of discovery and growth, and made us more in tune with who we are, but instead we were misled into creating alter egos and fake personas with illusions as lifestyles.

In order to connect with the Universe, God, Allah, etc., one must first be connected internally to one's own self, hence terms like *God helps those who help themselves*. Help yourself by reconnecting and disconnect yourself from the dysfunction that you are so used to. This will no doubt help you to discover a new you.

Anyway, I can't be bothered to talk about that topic anymore. I'll come back to that another time (yep, just like you I still have a bit of dysfunction going on in my head).

Right now, I'm looking at a beautiful butterfly and thinking to myself when the butterfly was a caterpillar. No-one cared about him, he was just a slow crawling piece of animal food, but now he's beautiful, and everyone loves him or her.
Basically, I'm saying no-one loves you or wants to help you on the come up, when you're grinding, trying to make a beautiful change, but the minute you become a successful butterfly, you're appreciated!

So be mindful of those new friends who only appreciate the butterfly. Make sure you keep an eye on the people who had respect for the caterpillar and cheered them on throughout the struggle.

#JustSayin'

Chapter 8

The Balance (God & the Devil): This is a topic that always strikes up a good conversation. Everyone thinks they were there when God created the world, their uncle Barry witnessed the whole thing, and they were passed down the knowledge (Okay…..).

And everyone thinks they know the devil; he has red skin, horns and lives in fire, near Hereford or, up (for debate), in Southend (but hey, who cares).

They have sold us some pretty amazing stories, and even given us pictures to match the stories, and us human beings have just accepted the stories without questioning anything (but hey, who I am I to say what you should believe?).
Me personally, I think in order to progress and be at peace with yourself, you must learn to work with both the bad and the good within you. You must appreciate both and make them co-exist as one.

OK, today is August 5th 2019. I wrote the above paragraph early in 2019 I think, and now I've come back to finish it but I really can't be bothered, I can't even remember why that topic came to my head about God and the devil. Damn, this is why when I get a vibe I've got to run with it straight away, otherwise I lose my focus. Other writers might read this and say, *This guy is taking the piss. What kinda writing is this?* And I'll respond by saying *This is more, me typing my direct thoughts inside my beautiful yet dysfunctional head, lol.*

OK, back to the whole love thing. Lately, I've been noticing that society and its system of pressure has made many people insecure, and society makes billions in cash from people's fear and insecurities.

Nobody seems to be happy; everybody is changing something (not that change is necessarily bad, change is amazing), but who are we trying to change for is the question. Are women and men changing their bodies for their personal love and comfort, or merely changing because of social pressure to look and be a certain way? Just something that crossed my mind, and as for me, I'm just plodding along through life, happy as fuck, looking like a rude boy (smile).

You see, there is beauty in imperfection, but it's a beauty that is often misunderstood and frowned upon, and a uniqueness that is always overlooked. Just like the kid in school who is always seen as disruptive, but maybe that kid just does not want to sit in your boring classroom. Maybe that kid has dreams and ambitions of playing baseball and he does not need a history lesson on Vikings to help him on his mission.

When we see the world through the energy of love, everything changes. You see everybody wants love, but lusting after and chasing love will only make love run away, but if you start to love yourself unconditionally, the energy of love will return to you and your surroundings.

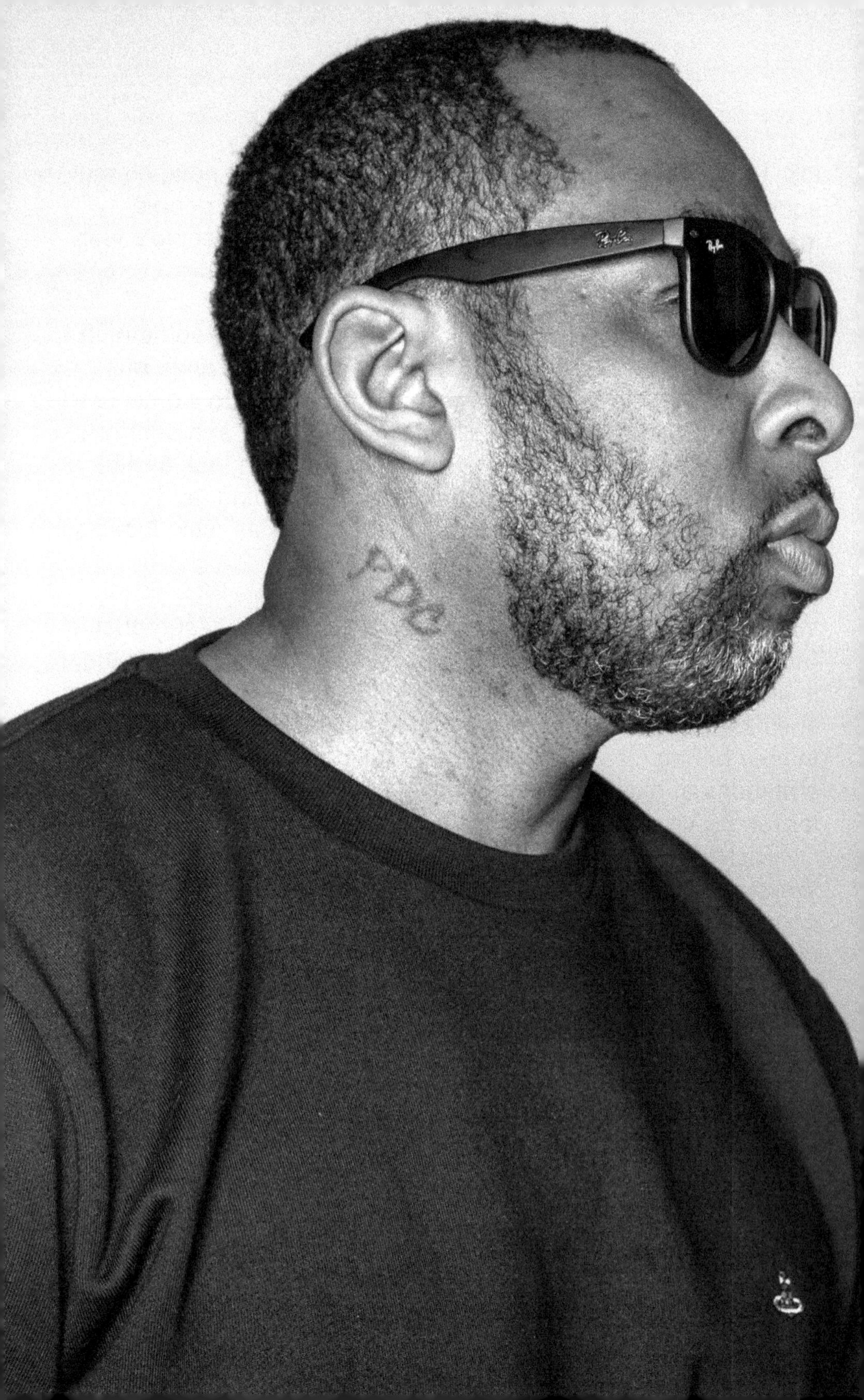
PDC

Within us is a deeper connection to outside.

I once asked a woman I know who was going through some depression and stress, *What are your flaws?* She replied, *I do not have any flaws, I am perfect.*

I looked at her in complete shock. I thought she was joking, but she was looking me dead in the eyes serious, and who am I to say someone is not perfect in their own world and through their own eyes, but damn, that is some real messed up shit.

Everyone has flaws, and if you think you're perfect, then anytime something imperfect happens to you, you're going to be stressed. So why not love the beauty of your imperfections, and instead of making them stress you out, why not work on putting so much love into the flaws, that those same flaws become flawless?

Boom! Now that is what I call the power of love.

The Dysfunction: Part 1

Dysfunction of thoughts in the mind! It's a deep topic that lots of people on the streets go through but do not understand. We grow up talking to ourselves, having discussions in our minds. At first it's just fun, we play with our toys, create makeshift worlds in our minds. But as we get older, we use the same creativity in the mind to explore and express our negative surroundings.

Our whole thought-process becomes negative, and in turn we invite that energy home and into our lives. Many people in these communities can't handle the voices that they themselves have created inside their own heads, along with the influence of the societies they live in. The very same creative voices and worlds they have planted in their minds so they can escape the real world, have become stronger and darker, and negativity starts to feed off their own fear. This can leave people feeling vulnerable, insecure and dysfunctional. Some even walk around talking out loud and in return are being labelled mentally ill, with many left in dodgy institutions to rot and get fed even more dodgy substances.

But what if those same negative voices and visions they created inside their own mind could be erased, and new voices and visions of love and positivity were replaced? That would mean many amazing people would be able to have a second chance at doing something progressive with their own life experience on Earth.
I just believe many of the problems we are facing can be adjusted or fixed, if people understood how important retraining the mind can be, especially when implementing the energy of love, into our thoughts and thinking patterns.

Chapter 9

The Magic of Music: So, I'm sitting in Mykonos in Greece, in a lovely villa apartment overlooking an amazing view of the sea and coastline. Hip-hop music is playing low in the background.

Listening, I start to drift off in my mind. I start to place scenes with the words the rapper is expressing to the audiences around the world. A whole music video is created in my head, with car chases, winning in life, and overcoming the struggle to create the most amazing lifestyle for myself.

Right then, I pause and think to myself, *Wow music is powerful, almost magical, How the words can put us in trance-like states and get embedded into our minds, and even have an influence on the way we behave and interact with others.*

Imagine listening to hardcore music all day that translates through rhythmic words, and melodic beats, screaming, murder, death, hate, struggle, kill, alcohol, take drugs, sex, sex, sex, money, etc. Over time, all this will become embedded in your subconscious mind.

For example, have you ever heard a song on the radio all day, and the next day at work you're sitting quietly - and boom, you start singing the same song you heard on radio the day before?
See, you don't even like the song, but you heard it so many times that the song got embedded in your subconscious, and you have memorised all the lyrics without even noticing. That's how powerful your mind is, and it also shows the magical influence music can have.

So, imagine the powerful effect music can have if it has an educational and progressive message! Imagine a progressive message being constantly stored in your subconscious mind, which in turn makes you constantly think about love, progressing, building, family, and other powerful words and thoughts? This would continue to have a massive impact on your life, your energy, your aura, and your daily life. Everything around us has an impact on the way we live and function.

As we listen, visualise and learn, our brains take in and store all the information, and then we use that information, often without knowing it, to form our reality. I have found that people from disadvantaged backgrounds often use music as a guide, advisor, mentor and escapism.

Sometimes music can work in your favour, but sometimes it can work against you.
That magical feeling music can give is amazing. You can be in a low-frequency mood, but then the lyrics, melody and vibe of the song raises you up and puts you in an amazing place, lightens up your entire day and changes the direction of your thinking.

This is what I call the magic of music.

Chapter 10

Her: (Well, this is more like a page of woman-worship, lol.) Today, I just want to admire her. She is amazing, she has many flaws yet she puts in the time and dedication to work on becoming a beautiful individual, aiming towards her highest potential. She is a woman, created and connected to the universe.

When I stare at her, I can't help but smile, my heart beats faster, and I think to myself, *Wow, look how powerful she is! A queen, a teacher, a mother, a sister, a daughter, a lover, and a partner; she is everything!*

She is modest, yet her sex appeal is like no other.
When I look into her eyes, I enter the universe, I feel the clouds, I see the sun, the moon, I see creation itself. I wonder does she know how powerful she really is? Does she understand what she is capable of?
The way she moves is so seductive yet she is unaware, because she is naturally sexy. I'm in awe of her.

I value her entire existence, I want to know more about her, I want to sit on a deserted beach on a tropical island and ask her questions, converse about life and the world, engage with her soul, speak to her inner child. I want to listen to her speak while gazing at her soft lips. It's crazy how men have made us believe it's A Man's World.
They don't even say a balanced world of both man and woman, but just straight, it's A Man's World. That is the biggest bullshit humanity has been presented with. For me, I'm going with the whole women lead, men protect vibe, because I think that's more productive and natural

In my opinion, a relationship needs to be based on the energy of love that fuels an amazing partnership, where both the man and women contribute to each other, with the aim of both of them being happy and reaching their highest potentials, and building an amazing world around themselves to then share with their future families.

Now, I'm on to thinking about wealth, health and happiness.

The Chase: I used to always be mad at myself, like why is nothing going right for me, why is life treating me so bad, then one day I sat down and had a reality check, a reflection. I sat down by myself and realised that I was chasing money. I was like a hamster running around in his wheel. I took a look and could see I was making bad choices, and the causes behind these choices were having an effect on my life.

From that day forward, I stopped chasing, and focused on building a better me, a better way of thinking, and most importantly, making better choices.

I had come to realise I was chasing passions and ego dreams instead of focusing on my natural gift and this was why things were going wrong in my life. All I had to do was channel and work on my gift. From that day on, my life started changing.

You see, your gift is your natural talent, and all you have to do is enhance it and your whole life will change.

Find your own gift, work on it and you will start to feel happier than you have ever been.

3rd Eye Love: Looking at life via love gives you a whole different view of life, and a new experience with people and the way you interact with different situations.
We must not only look for love inside us all, we must learn to feel the love.

Imagine being able to come out of your body and looking back at yourself. What changes would you make? Write them down and start working towards the changes straight away.

Love is not like a box of chocolates (that was just a way to sell you over-priced chocolates). Love is much deeper than anything in the physical. Love is an energy, a vibration, a frequency, and when you discover how to embrace and channel love, you will then be able to share it.

Dont just say Love Be Love.

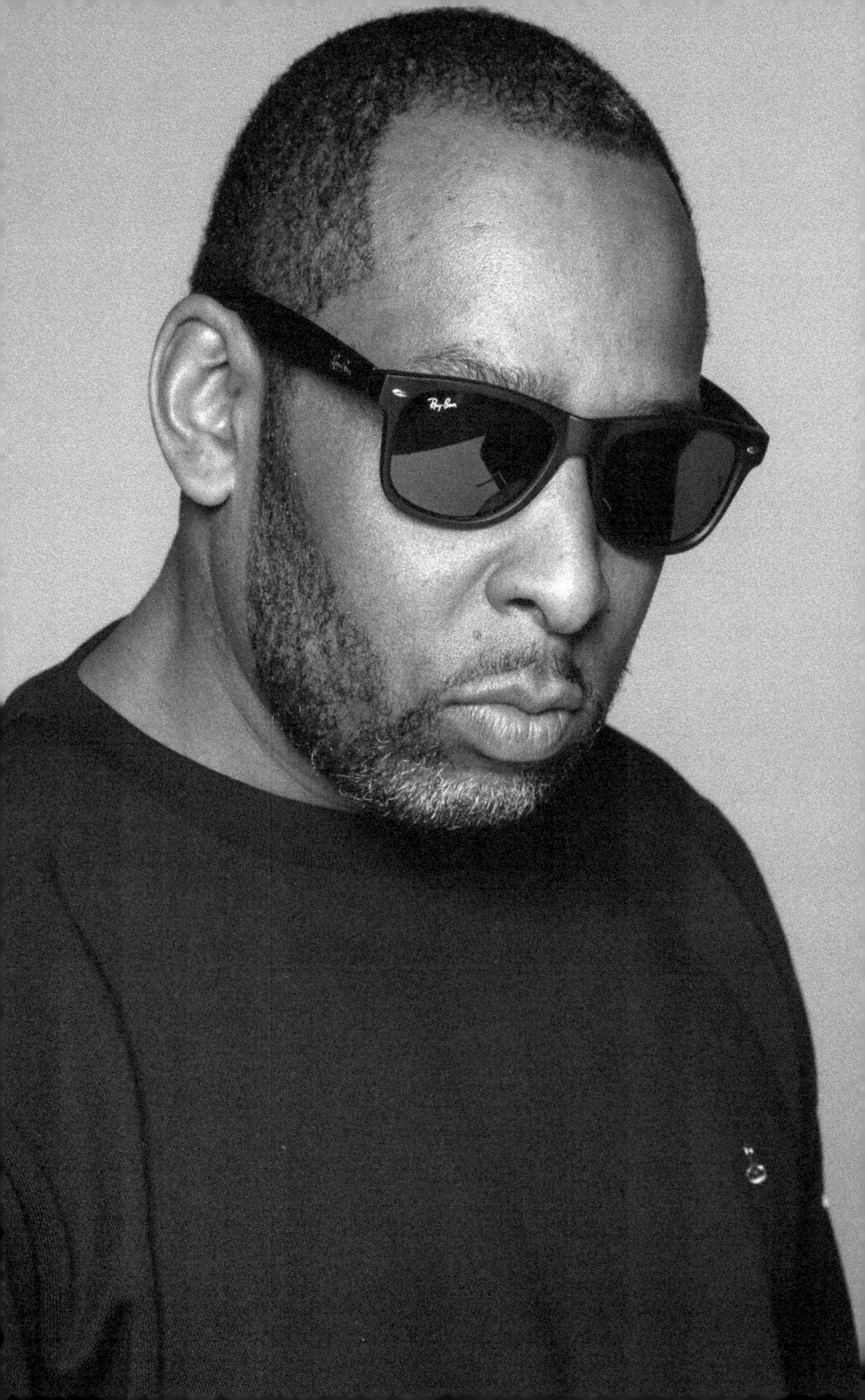
Ray-Ban

Chapter 11

My Brother the Street: People always ask me what it's like living on the streets. I think these people see the streets as some great fun place, where everyone's living this amazing criminal lifestyle with fancy cars and drug dealing and designer clothes. They go out to amazing parties and live in nice houses smoking weed, and everything is so great.

Then I hit them with the reality, like, *Do you know that it is a very stressful and unhappy lifestyle on the street, and that 80% of street culture live unhappy and the majority of people on estates are very sad? It's not a great environment.*

Like, we live in a place where you can just about see over the buildings, as everything is always high, and tower blocks are everywhere. On the streets, you're always surrounded by high buildings growing up. This is a very unhappy environment, our families are poor and broken, and living in bad circumstances.

We didn't sell drugs for the fun of it. We sold drugs because there was no food in the cupboard for real, or there was no way of us getting school uniform etc. That's why we do these things. And again, we do it because we live in such bad environments and low-income circumstances, and we do our best to make these bad situations look good. Being like that can sometimes come across as if we are showing off about how great our lives are, but I can tell you this is far from the truth.

No one wants to be here. No one really likes living in poverty, it is not a nice life. We're all trying to get out, we're all trying to do something so we can actually leave this place and buy our mums a better house, buy our Dad a better house, plus houses for our families so they can be in better conditions to raise their children.

A lot of people will also see us in our flash cars, flash music videos and think that our life is great. No, we are just trying to show people a life that we want to live. You see, no-one's happy here.
And that's the main thing, people forget that this is not the life we chose.

Most of us didn't choose these surroundings, or the streets environment. We just made the best out of the environment that we lived in. We don't want to go to prison because we already know we have been imprisoned in our own minds already, so why would anyone want to go into prison?
We are just making the best out of a really bad situation, so we put it into our music and into our films, not glamorizing it, just showing it as a way of life, but sometimes this can come across as glamorizing the criminal lifestyle.

My main aim was always to have a big house with a luxury swimming pool, living good while riding my motorbike in the sun, up in the mountain roads. I would be driving expensive cars, and flying around in private jets and helicopters and living an amazing life.

I've never wanted to stay in the ghetto or go to prison or sell drugs my whole life.

And for a lot of the young people out on the streets, that wasn't their plan either. You see, we are very talented individuals, but we just do not have the support or the platforms usually, to bring our dreams into a reality. You see, a lot of the young people on the streets who are labelled as being hard to reach, disadvantaged etc., are very spiritual and emotional, really connected people, who have not had the right opportunities that can help them reach their highest potential.

To add fuel to the fire, the schooling system, and the way that they teach is not for us. Many young people have entrepreneurial attitudes, and school does not endorse, prepare, or build on these types of attitudes, in many young people. It does not benefit us, and we do not relate to a lot of the formulas that they put in front of us. So therefore, when we do leave school, we end up in worse situations because we haven't been properly prepared.

And not helping us to be prepared is just as bad as the education system that sets us up to fail.

So, imagine there are some people on the streets, like old school gangsters and original O.G.z, and they've been on the streets for like 30 to 40 years. Some of them don't even own a house, they have no assets, or business or savings, and no proper family structure. Can you picture being on the streets all these years, going through prison battles, drugs, fights, stress, losing close friends, gang violence, and so many more problems on the streets? And they are going through all of this for no reason, but to end up with nothing at all except for war stories that have no relevance or benefit to you, your people, or community.

This is a major part of the story that a lot the young people don't get to hear about or see. This is the true story for 80% of respected O.G.z.

The importance of ownership and the building of the family structure is key to the growth and development of any people.

And most importantly, to see and feel things through love. We, as a street culture, have seen a lot of things from the viewpoint of violence and anger, and it hasn't got us anywhere except the graveyard and prison, or leaving us as victims of drug use.

The street community needs to start seeing things from a different angle. The streets need to start working together. Imagine what we can achieve working as a team, as a community! We could achieve so much.

For instance, in the street community, we have music, which is a big part of our community. But imagine if we owned our own music. If we owned our own music industry, we would be in a much better position to help our young people.

Hip hop, street rap and grime and most of the most popular music styles have come from our community. If we were able to come together to own, organize and structure our own music industry, we would gain wealth and be able to build better platforms for our young people and bring a more sustainable wealth back into our communities. We would then be in a great position to build and help our other brothers and sisters in other countries.

You see, this is how the power of love works; it's about us realizing our full potential, and then going out and sharing the love so other people can also realize their full potential. See, by working together as a team we can build better futures and a better environment for all of us. On the streets, a lot of the young people grow up without any love, and no proper family structures, and they think prison is a part of their natural life, and that dying at 21 is normal - well nowadays dying at 15 seems to be normal!

Chapter 12

The Interview: So today I'm being interviewed by a young female journalist. She knows I am writing about love and has come to ask me some questions, so it's only right I add it into this lovely book.

Anyway I'm sitting in a comfortable leather chair as she walks into the room wearing a lovely dress, with nice sliders on her feet. I look straight at her toes they are clean, tidy and cute. I love women with nice toes (Errmm, Elijah concentrate). Her hair is up in a tight ponytail, her face is smooth yet she has on no makeup. She's a natural beauty.

She puts her hand out to greet me. *Hi, my name is Nicole.* As she moves to sit down, I can smell her perfume. She smells really nice, I'm impressed.

She gets straight to the point as if she can feel I'm slyly checking her out.

So, Elijah, nice to finally meet you. What's with your big interest on the love topic?
Well Nicole, I believe the key to a beautiful life and reaching our highest potential lies in the power of love.
For a second our eyes locked to each other. She looked away and said *Why do you think people are so scared to tap into love?*

I replied, *People do not understand love. Love has been packaged and sold back to the people as a Valentine present, roses and chocolates. We have been told to be strong and heartless because love is for weak and soft people.*

We have not been taught to feel love, express or share love, and then make the love grow to help us reach our full potential.
She stared at me and smiled, *Wow that's pretty, really deep stuff. So how did you start your journey to the power of love Elijah?*

I explained, *I had started to realise that I was always putting myself around angry and negative environments and situations, but felt totally comfortable in it. I was addicted to chaos. My mindset was an angry one. I was angry at everyone and everything, and I blamed everyone for my downfalls in life. I had no connection to the love energy because on the streets, that kind of stuff was frowned upon.*

I started to look at my life in depth, and realised it was my mindset that was causing me problems in life, so I needed to change the way I thought and felt. I needed to appreciate and be more grateful, I needed to tap into love in order to grow and see and feel things differently and more progressively. While I spoke I could feel Nicole's eyes looking straight through me and hugging my mind.

She realised she was staring for too long and quickly turned away.

Blushing, she said *Can you excuse me while I quickly go to the ladies room please?*

Cool, I said. *No problem.*

Look straight into her soul.

As she got up and started walking away, I found myself staring at her beautiful body shape and wondered if she was wearing any underwear, or if she had on a sexy G-string.

As she reached the door, she turned slyly and caught me looking at her. *Damn*, I thought to myself. *Stay focus Jaj, and stop being disrespectful!*

But yes, I still have a lot of work to do on myself, I'm a work in progress, still not perfect, lol (lol means Laugh Out Loud to all you aliens). After a while she came back into the room, smiled and sat back down on the chair opposite me. She looked very beautiful and I wondered if she knew how beautiful she was, and how powerful her presence is, so me being me, I asked her.

Hey Nicole, are you aware of how beautiful you are? She looked caught off guard with the question, then she replied, *Why, thank you.*

But I then said to her, *As much as it was a compliment, it was also a direct question.* She smiled and said, *Well not really, I'm just me.*

I looked at her and said, *What do you mean you're just you? Don't you look in the mirror everyday smile to yourself and think, damn I'm beautiful?* She giggled, blushed and said, *No.*
Well Nicole, I stand in the mirror every morning and I say to myself "Jaj, you're the man, you handsome bastard!"
Nicole burst out laughing. *You are really something else.*

Anyway, Nicole said, all serious again, like she just remembered this was supposed to be her interview. *If a man loves a woman, why would he take advantage of her? And does true love make you want to be a better version of yourself?*

Okay, I replied. *Regarding your first question, a man can only take advantage of a woman if she is willing to give him the energy and space to take advantage of her. But on the flip side even when we were kids, haven't we charmed and lied to get our own way? As you know, people need love so much that they sometimes give love to a person who is taking advantage of them all the time.*

Love is not painful, in my opinion those types of traits should be put with insecurity, and low-frequency energy. You cannot say you are taking advantage of someone because you love them. Love does not take advantage of people; instead it embraces, comforts, enlightens and helps to build people towards their highest potential.

And for your second question, the energy of true love will bring you freedom, and with freedom you will be able to see clearly with no distractions or misdirection. You will be able to focus and move forward in the direction you wish to go, and tap into a new vibration of energy inside yourself. You can become one with your mind body and soul, and in my opinion that will make you be a better version of yourself.

With that answer, Nicole stared intensely at me for a while, then smiled and said, *Thank you.* The interview was at peace.

The Social Media Rant: I'm in a room filled with loads of different people. Out of about 30 of them, 25 are stuck to their phones, and the other 5 are looking around like, *What the hell am I doing here?* I'm one of the 5.

Wow, it's like we have been hypnotised. People are addicted to their phones and its apps, and it's like a real-life, online crack epidemic. How did we become so consumed by social media? I wonder, if we looked at love the same way, would we then be in a different world?

What if people put that same energy into love, thinking love, being love and giving love - what then? I bet some of you are thinking, *No way! That would be like a weird Utopian love world, HA HA!*

OK, well, I didn't mean it to sound so dull and strange, like in the movies where everyone wears white and there's no crime or swearing etc., that would be real crap. We all need a bit of dysfunctional behaviour now and again lol.

But anyway, back to what I was saying. Imagine that same amount of energy we use on social media was also used as a love energy. Imagine using that energy to learn more about yourself and retrain your mindset out of old, bad habits that are also having a bad impact on your life.

Not saying social media is bad, coz everyone loves a swipe and a DM now and again, lol (a little stroke of the ego every other week ain't too bad, I suppose).

But just imagine how amazing it would be if the misdirection they throw at us via social media and the other social crap society throws at us, was taken and used as tools to tap into our subconscious to help us reach our higher potentials and tap into better frequencies? #JustSayin'

Chapter 13

The Dysfunction: Part 2

Growing up in a hostile, dysfunctional environment can have a really bad effect on our mindset, and without truly knowing why, many of us have created our own inner demons.

We have created monsters in our minds and in return, we reflect those same monsters into our own reality. We create or manifest what we think, and therefore because we grow up in environments that are openly described as being poor or disadvantaged, we take on the embodiment of that responsibility without really understanding the effects of that conditioning.

Growing up on an estate, I was constantly told I was living in the ghetto. I was struggling, I was a child of the struggle, I was from a bad estate, my people were slaves, and that most of our family members were in prison. Society groomed me to think and grow negative.

So in return, even though my core principles and knowledge of myself and my heritage taught to me by my parents was rich, wealthy and powerful, I started to say I'm from the ghetto, I started to believe that I was poor and struggling. I believed the world was against me, so I created a demon to protect myself. I created a hard, defensive, strong alter-ego a menace to society, a fighter, a soldier to fight a war, but what war was I fighting? There was no war. It was all an illusion, a lie, a misdirection, a concept built to misguide my mind - and I fell for it.

So now imagine, four billion people on Earth have been tricked and misguided, just as I was. These four billion humans have also created demons in their minds and have attracted it into their reality. Just think of the negative influence this concept of struggle and poverty has given to the world!

The Earth has enough food, water and resources for everyone, so there is no poverty. Poverty is a concept, a thought and nothing more. Men have realised the power they can gain by making you think poor, then sell you the idea of being rich. By doing this, they can control probably the most precious thing we have - the mind.

The demons we have created within our minds have caused so many unnecessary problems in our day to day life, and have messed up our relationships. For example (and here goes another dramatic example, lol).

The demon we have created looks at a woman from the physical only. We are attracted only to a women's arse, boobs or other body parts when we are in that demon mode. We choose our partners in demon mode and sooner or later a baby is created. But that's when the demon disappears for a bit and our eyes open and at that point, we realise that we don't really like this woman, and we didn't really want a baby, especially with that woman.

Actually, there's really nothing you like about her apart from her fat arse when she's bent over in doggy position (damn, that's harsh Jaj). Yeah it's harsh but it's true and very sad as this will continue a negative cycle of sadness, dysfunction and a poverty mindset.

You see the demon in men we create is greedy, selfish, dark, unloving, and only concerned with making sure the world knows who we are and that we are seen and heard. That's its primary goal; it is shallow and selfless and does not care who or what is hurt on the way.

Women create demons in themselves too, and the demon in a woman is just as fierce. A woman will be angry, angry at her Dad, and angry at men in general because society has taught her that men are evil, savage, and they will hurt you. She will then create a demon to defend her against such evil. Her demon will be aggressive, independent, and it will create a plan of how her family will look, the type of man she wants, the kids' names and ages etc. The demon has it all planned out, and she will finally meet a man that she thinks will suit her plan of action.

Meanwhile, the man is oblivious to all of this. He just thinks he's on a lovely date, but little does he know that the demon has plans for him regardless of what he wants. The guy has no plans to start a family, and he lets her know this. She smiles inside her mind, they have amazing sex and he gets lost in the moment with no condom. She smiles as he sends shivers all the way into her womb, and the demon smiles from inside knowing this will create chaos, poverty and dysfunction, continuing the cycle that society needs in order to control and misdirect.

The mind is so powerful, but we are never taught how powerful the mind is and how we can use it better.

We are taught to think according to what society believes. We are taught to believe in religions and concepts that society thinks is good for us. Higher powers (here he goes again with his conspiracy theories), they all know the power of free thinking and how thoughts can become a reality, and they know how beautiful and powerful our individual minds are.

To help ourselves, we just need to learn how powerful the mind is. We need to retrain and rethink our thoughts, change our habits and patterns, especially those of us who come from local estates and so called disadvantaged areas.
We need to kill the, *I'm struggling* type of thinking, the, *I'm from the ghetto* mentality, the *I can only be a drug dealer,* thoughts, the *I must go prison in order to be cool and real* mentality, we need to drop this out!

We need to get rid of the poverty ego. We need to kill the demon within, and replace it with love and amazing thoughts of progress, inspiration, health, wealth, helping others and contributing to the incredible human life on Earth.

Over the years, I have seen the demon mentality destroy the mindsets of some of the most beautiful and intelligent people from my community through constant worry and struggle-thinking. They became poisoned with the bitterness and anger that they have been feeding their demon daily.

I tell many young people, *Be careful what you think and be mindful of what you make your reality. You have the power to be anything you want, so make your reality positive and progressive. Don't make society tell you how you should live or think.*

In everything we do, there will always be struggles and hardship as that comes with building greatness, but we must not trap our minds into thinking we struggle with unhappiness by default, because this is not true. We are simply part of a struggle or unhappiness due to the way we think, and the concepts we were taught.

Think Great: Imagine waking up in the morning, smiling and saying to yourself, *Today I'm going to have an amazing day.* And then thinking, *I'm grateful for the life that I have, I'm happy, I'm blessed, I'm beautiful, and I am great.*

If we constantly tell ourselves these kinds of things, we will influence our subconscious to act on them and send that same energy out to the world. We then become what we think.

This is a very powerful and beneficial concept. No wonder they didn't teach us about ourselves in school - they needed robots not free thinkers. #JustSayin'
See, we are not taught about the power of love, or the power of the mind. In fact, we are not even taught about the powers we possess as human beings! We are taught to be scared, to fear, fear not getting a job, fear not getting the right grades, fear not meeting the right partner, fear of being unsuccessful. Everything is fucking fear!

But I'm here to tell you all, especially my young people on the streets, *Do not fear! You are all individually great!* Life is about learning, growing, reaching and understanding your full potential, and it doesn't matter where you are from. Rich, poor, religious, atheist, black, white, green or blue, we all have the potential to shine, grow and be amazing at anything we choose to do.

Most people are unhappy because they have given their mind, their thinking, their love, to the system, to society. We are not in control, we have become like puppets, slaves to the higher powers in charge, we no longer think for ourselves, and our minds are constantly being manipulated and misdirected.

If you are reading this, my advice to you is - *From this moment, retrain and rethink, re-program your mind, change your subconscious paradigm and THINK GREAT.*

The Conversation in my Head: I have regular conversations with myself. Maybe I'm like a thin line between sane and insane, who knows, but I see it as a beautiful thing even though, if I told you everything that goes on in my head, I'd probably get myself sectioned, lol.

Anyway, today me and my head are discussing whether or not I should cut off my friends circle and start the new year totally fresh. I'm thinking maybe to cut off a few, and keep a few, but my head is like, *Nah, forget that. Let's cut them all off and move forward.*

But I'm trying to tap into my love energy and be a bit compassionate, but my head is like, *Fuck that Elijah. If you love yourself and others, you would do what's best for you and move towards your full potential. If you stay around the same people, you will get the same results.*

This made me think; Do we as people hold onto the wrong kind of love thinking it's the right kind of love, when really we are doing ourselves more harm than good?

Imagine how many people on the streets around the world, are still around their longtime friends thinking it's out of loyalty or love, when really, it's just become a habit or a pattern that they have become used to, when they could have achieved more by being around a more beneficial circle of friends someplace else?

Now, with the power of love energy, I started looking at people I called friends, and studying their character, behaviour, and vibration. Do they inspire or motivate me? Are they happy for me when I win? Are they supportive of me when I lose?

This questioning is something I believe each one of us should do on a regular basis in order to keep a good frequency of people around us that benefit our potential and vibe.
Now my head was going full scale. If it was up to my head, I would be living on a mountain far from human beings totally isolated and by myself, lol.

Anyway, I'm grateful I have a balance because I have a head and a heart, so I use both even though the heart can get me into problems sometimes.

Also, my heart will say something like, *No, give your friends a chance. They might not be doing anything now, but maybe in 10 years they will change.* And I'm like, *What, 10 years? Flipping heck, and you want me to stay around them and be uninspired for 10 years? Wow!*

So, this is my daily battle as I wake up. My head and heart is like the Bloods and the Crips (once again for the detail freaks, Bloods and Crips are two gangs in America who don't always like each other).

But after I had a deep think, I was actually 70/30 towards agreeing with my head. Sometimes you have to be cruel to be kind in order to be happy and make progress in your life.

Some people may be thinking, *How do you just remove yourself from your old friends circle?* It's simple.

You can either move to your new desired area and don't see them again, or just buy a new phone and start immediately hanging around people you want to grow with.

And remember, you can always come back for them once you are successful or happier. It's not the end of the world; it's more like the beginning of something great.

Random Head Moment: I was meditating this morning and having a peaceful vibe, when my head interrupted the vibe like, *Yo, what's good bro?*
I was like, *Flipping heck, can't you let me meditate in peace?* My head was like, *Nah forget all that sitting down stuff creating new patterns in your subconscious. Let's hit the road and make some money.*

I was just about to have an argument (this is a regular thing by the way), but I just remembered, why am I arguing with my head, when I'm the one who is in control, not my head!. You see, sometimes we forget that we are in control of ourselves, but what has happened over time is that we have created bad patterns inside our heads, We have created bad habits influenced by our environment, and what we listen to and see on a regular basis, and this has had an effect on our minds and behaviour. It also makes the head think it can do what it wants.

Do not let your mind wander off and dictate what and who you are. Take control, and make sure your mind and heart is working for you - not against you.

Sometimes all we need is silence.

Insecurities: Lately, I have been noticing how so many people's daily routine revolves around insecurities that they have picked up from society and experiences like their past and current relationships.
But do we realise we are living our life via insecurity? I say *we*, because I also get caught up in my ego and insecurity at times, so don't worry, I'm not preaching. Sometimes, I'm as messed up as you are, lol.

Let me give you an example; the other day I was talking with my friend about women and he says, *The majority of women are slags*. I replied swiftly like, *Bro, that is a bit harsh and not quite true, because you do not know the majority of women in society, so that statement is a bit flawed.*

Really, he was basing his opinion on his own personal experience with his past girlfriend, or other women he had met and encountered a bad experience with. When I said this to him, he got upset and said I was
defending slags.

I looked him in the eyes and I could see a hurt, a pain, that was hitting his soul, so while I was talking to him, he was probably remembering a bad experience with those women and in turn bringing that energy into the present conversation.

I started thinking, *Imagine how many of us are doing similar things to what my friend was doing.*
We are bringing our past negative experiences with us into our future and basing our thoughts, opinions and mindset around our insecurities.

Once you base your thoughts on insecurity, you are living and thinking on a low-frequency, and you will be vibrating on the experience of what created the insecurity in the first place. For example (I do examples because when you're from the street, your brain takes things in better when it's broken into an example or a picture. That is just because we are special people, God's favourites, and all, lol.)

Anyway, say you have a fight and you lose, you can either tell yourself that you win some you lose some, take it as a positive life lesson, and turn it into a positive vibe, or you can get angry and hold a silent hatred for the other person. What that last choice will do is, every time you remember the fight you will remember the hatred, and bring forward that same energy and create a new insecurity.

Basically, what I am saying is we need to be more careful with how we are letting our insecurities play a major role in our thinking and thought process. We need to understand better what we are basing our wants and needs around, and what the driving force is behind the energy we are putting out into the world that we are creating for ourselves.

Do not let insecurities direct your love and energy. BOOM!

The Inner Voice or Intuition: Many of us have felt an energy within us, that speaks to us, reminds us, warns us and looks out for us. Some people say it's God, some say it's Jesus, and some say it's our subconscious. Others say it's an angel and a demon, and that we have a choice which to listen to, but some say it's our spiritual guide. All I know is, whatever it is, it's fucking awesome.

Once you tap into your intuition, your whole life can change because it can help build your confidence and character. People always ask, *What is the big secret, how do you tap in?* I say, *Just practice silence, listen and learn.*

Forgiveness: I was just randomly thinking, as I do (and by now you definitely know I am a random thinker). Imagine just forgiving everyone that's ever done you bad. Imagine waking up and saying to yourself, *Today, I forgive everyone and everything. I am no longer mad or upset with anybody. I even forgive myself.*

Do you know how powerful that is for the mind?
Doing that will instantly start to transform the way you think and look at life. Remember that kid in nursery that broke your favourite toy, and for 25 years you have been thinking, *If I could go back in time, I would punch that kid right in the nose*. Or the female who caught her guy cheating 10 years ago, still thinks to herself, *I wish I would have kicked him harder in the balls, he deserves one more arse whooping!*

Just think of all the years of negative experiences we have harnessed into our minds, anger going round and round in circles and creating our energy for us inside our subconscious mind. Just imagine thinking about all of them for one last time, and instead of being upset, just smile and forgive. Wow, what a great feeling.

It took me until I was a grown man to understand the power of forgiveness. I used to always hear about forgiveness coming from religious people, and sometimes they can be real jarring, so I didn't really take it in how I should have, but hey it's never too late.

The universe has a language that can be translated through intuition.

Imagine going to see your Dad who has not seen you or called you in the past ten years, and instead of being angry, you walk up to him and say, *I forgive you*. Do you know how beneficial that will be for you?

Life can sometimes have us just gathering up anger for things that are not really that bad, things that we could easily have forgiven and moved on in life.
And most importantly, we must forgive ourselves for mistakes we have made along the way during our life journey. Truss me, it's not that bad, try it sometime.

I was just thinking to myself that lately I've been feeling a bit unsettled. Have you ever tried to think, but you just end up with a headache? It happens when our minds get noisy, and we are constantly cluttering our minds with social bullshit, bills, and the mainstream news. All this stuff just attacks and chills in our minds, and creates a busy atmosphere in our head, making it more difficult for us to think.

So, I guess all I am saying is sometimes we need to be more mindful of what we are cluttering our mind with.

Starting over new, from scratch, sounds scary to a lot of people but it is probably one of the most important things you can do in your life to help you move forward and grow. Many people out there in the world are stuck, feeling trapped like their whole world is just constantly going round in circles. I believe when your life gets to this point, that the universal energy is trying to tell you that it's time for a change. This is not a bad thing, it means your current life or lifestyle is coming to an end, and that there is a new door open, ready for you to walk through.

Now, this is the scary part, walking through an open door and you do not know where it will lead you to, is what holds most people back in life.

I heard the biggest opportunities are on the other side of fear, and I understand why someone would say this. Do not be scared to change for the better. Take the leap of faith, and do not be afraid to start over. Change is Growth.

My Cousin called me today from prison, he is doing a 25-year sentence. He said to me on the phone that now he actually knows what an appreciation for little things in life feels like.

It's crazy how things like walking through the park are not really appreciated until you can no longer walk freely into the park. This made me think. We have to continuously remind ourselves to be grateful for the little things we have because simple things are some of the most precious things we will experience.

I just felt someone out there right now needs to read this.

Be Great Be the F**king Greatest:
I have written my personal thoughts down in this book not only in the hope that it will motivate and inspire at least one person, but to show people that we all have flaws, crazy personalities and that we all make many mistakes that we can learn from.
I wrote my thoughts down in the rawest form to show you my normality, my in the shower talking to myself moments, my true self with no frills; just the energy of love. I wanted to share with you my opinions and experiences of love, a love that we were not introduced to by society, a love that even some of our parents didn't understand.

I want you to know that we are the diamonds that have been covered in shit, and looked down upon by society as the smell, the disease, the infection, the problem, the unloved. But underneath all the chaos and dysfunction, we are still diamonds, the most precious on the planet.

Do not be afraid to wash away the shit society has stained us with via our environments and social conditioning. Reclaim your diamond-self, wash away the shit from your mind, and instead cover yourself with a protective layer of love, and shine brighter than ever before, and never EVER dim your light for anybody ever again.

Find and tap into the love that is so powerful inside you, that it immediately transforms the entire life outside of you.

For Nasir, Saadiq, Kenya, Nairobi and Maasai

The Power Of Love

Do not underestimate the power of your thoughts and feelings.

Jaja Soze

Lightning Source UK Ltd.
Milton Keynes UK
UKHW020635230921
391069UK00011B/782